Story De

Storyteller's Handbook for Writers & Dream Merchants

by Shared Experience Art Machine

Published by
Shared Experience Art Machine

ISBN 978-0-9573558-1-1

PART ONE
INTRODUCTION

Who is this book for?

This book is for anyone who has a story to sell.

You might be a novelist, a screenwriter, an editor, a publisher, a creative producer - or, even, a marketer. It doesn't matter. Either way, you want to tell - and sell - your story well.

It is a book for Dream Merchants.

All the examples used in this book relate to screenwriting. Our approach and methodology is based on a lifetime of experience from our SEAM mentors - years of story pitching, development and sales. Nevertheless, the methods that we use are applicable to all forms of fictional storytelling. We know this because the authors of this handbook have worked on films, plays, novels, short stories, websites, video games, and transmedia projects - all of which wanted to sell their stories to the public. The objective is the same, even if the medium is not.

The methods that we employ create better stories by design. After that, it's up to you. Whether or not you deliver a killer app, screenplay, or video game relies upon many factors but we will give you a solid foundation that will put you ahead of most of your competition.

If you want to discuss, debate, or put into practice anything that you read in this book - then please visit our online community: Shared Experience Art Machine (www.seam.tv). There, you will find a specific group devoted to this book (www.seam.tv/groups/story-design) - and, also, a community of like-minded artists and creative consumers who have come together to create great storytelling franchises of the future.

Who We Are

SEAM (Shared Experience Art Machine) is a community of Artists that exchange ideas, techniques, and best practices in order to create new transmedia franchises for the future. Our board of advisors have worked on many feature films - both for major Hollywood studios and for independent distribution. They have been involved in the creation of this book in order to share their knowledge and develop a handbook for storytellers. The methodology outlined in this book is the foundation of all, new project development at SEAM. We hope that it helps storytellers around the world to develop better stories by design.

For more information on SEAM, please visit www.seam.tv/about

Storytelling is for us a passion as much as it is a career. We learn a great deal from our development process and we continue to learn more each and every time we work on a new story project. Perhaps storytelling is a form of therapy, because we discover all of our own hopes, fears, failures and dreams in the process. But it's hard work. And it can easily become overwhelming which is why we have distilled the story creation process down to seven steps which we outline in this book.

If you are a writer, then we advocate that you find a good creative producer or story editor. The reason being that they are adept at seeing the forest for the trees. They know what is required to tell a good story - even if they cannot write one themselves. It is an important partnership. If you are writer, then you need to ally yourself with someone who believes in your skill but who can give you unabashed and constructive criticism. Someone who knows where to invest your time to make the story better. Someone who is mindful of the marketplace and what makes for both good business and good entertainment. You will find these people on SEAM.

This book is short and to the point. The more we say, the less you'll probably remember anyway. We believe that we have developed a simple, common-sense approach to storytelling that many writers here at SEAM have found helpful. Hopefully, you will feel the same way. If so, we encourage you to join our SEAM community (www.seam.tv). There, you will find a forum for best practices for all of us to exchange ideas, advice and insights. We are doing this because we are passionate about storytelling. Without good stories, we have nothing. Our world would be empty and meaningless. Storytellers are the lifeblood of our industry and contribute to our understanding of the human condition.

There are many how-to writing books. However, there are only a few that we draw from heavily in our book.
Here they are:
"The Art of Dramatic Writing" by Lajos Egri
"The Moral Premise: Harnessing Virtue & Vice for Box Office Success" by Stanley D. Williams

If you are a screenwriter, you might also enjoy:
"The Screenwriter's Bible: A Complete Guide to Writing, Formatting, and Selling Your Script" by Dave Trottier

Everything else is experience… You must write, and write often.

PART TWO
STORY DESIGN

Start Writing by Not Writing

Storytelling may not be the oldest profession on earth (so they say!) but it's certainly been around as long as language itself. Over the years it has become highly commercialised - a commodity, even. According to Wikipedia, there are over a million books published around the world every year. A new screenplay is completed every minute. Over 100,000 are penned every year in the US alone. Only 5,000 of those make it to film markets… 600 of which are picked up for production. Even less actually make it to the finish line and far fewer are distributed. As for their profitability, nobody knows for sure, except that the top ten films of the year take over half of all the box office receipts, despite representing only 2% of the script market.

The world is full of screenplays. Most of them badly written. This wouldn't be such a problem if they remained hidden in a drawer somewhere… but they don't. They end up on the desks of executives - like ours - or, more frequently, screened by an army of readers employed to filter out the dross. We're not complaining, because panning for gold is part of the job. But we think it is unfortunate, because a lot of time, energy and talent goes into writing a screenplay - even a bad one.

The truth is, good work is rare. And we mean 'good' not 'great'. Great work is a four-leaf clover. We'd settle for good. Good work is rare because most people lack the discipline and passion to make a difference. Talent is a given. You can't get anywhere without it. But talent isn't the ultimate driver of success. Instead, it comes down to craftsmanship and gumption. Both take time to nurture and must be regularly exercised. It doesn't matter that you wrote a fantastic manuscript today, if you cannot deliver another good one tomorrow. Success demands repeatability. How often can you deliver high quality work to a deadline - again and again? That is the question.

Craftsmanship and efficiency - that's what this book is about: helping storytellers to construct better stories as efficiently as possible. And in order to do this - you will need a framework.

There are many forms of storytelling but this book is written primarily with the screenwriter in mind. That said, the approach that we are advocating is applicable to other forms of writing that adhere to classical storytelling structures. The reason being that the tools used to construct a great story-design also provide a solid architecture - irregardless of the final form of execution. And, ultimately, audiences have long been steeped in the storytelling traditions of the cinema, which means that these have had a profound impact on all other storytelling forms.

The reason that there is so much poor material in circulation, we believe, is that writers often start writing instead of designing. They have an idea and they can't wait to get cracking. Or, they've been thinking about their story for a long time in their minds and figure that they will sort out the niggly details after they get started. In either case, they don't spend sufficient time designing their story before they begin.

The problem with this approach is that you solidify your thoughts too early in the process. You fall in love with your characters, favourite scenes, witty bits of dialogue... and you paint yourself into a corner. When you realise that things aren't working out, you have to fight against the urge to protect what you've written - all that hard work. It's very unusual for a writer to happily scrap everything and start again. So, we are going to suggest another way. Instead of writing, you spend your time planning. You think about critical elements of your story design and structure, before you even fashion your characters, or plot. Put story design first.

Another reason for focusing on story design first is to be flexible. In the beginning, it's just you and a blank screen. But at some point in the process other people get involved. And they won't shut up. And you can't tell them to either, because they'll have money, distribution, contacts and lots of other resources you will need to get your story in front of an audience. They will give you reams and reams of notes. They will change their minds. They will be frustrated writers - like many creative producers - who lack the discipline to do what you do well. So, you will need to be ready to deal with all these people and their suggestions. If you have a well-designed story, then you can afford to be flexible. For instance, if half-way through the process they decide that the genre needs to be changed because the current one isn't working many lesser writers might have a melt-down (or, possibly, a nervous breakdown). They would be afraid that it would mess with their story and it would require enormous amounts of re-writing. However, if you have a good story design, you will be able to embrace their suggestion as a good idea or, alternatively, argue effectively against it. The reason being that the story isn't determined by the genre. What?? That's right. Because you rigorously developed the story design, you will know how to alter the expression of the narrative as required - without destroying your underlying story. If you hadn't done this work up front, then you could very easily lose the story in the process. And, also, lose your mind.

Perhaps you think that planning is the antithesis to innovation - that it interrupts the flow of creativity? If so, we would like to convince you otherwise. In fact, we find that when we are limited by choice - when we are forced to work within the confines of a narrow set of rules - we actually outperform. Starting with a completely blank sheet of paper is the same as facing infinite possibility and unlimited choice. It isn't helpful. It's overwhelming. If you've ever hunted for breakfast cereal in the aisles of an American supermarket, you'll know what we're talking about. There is simply too much choice. Too much choice kills creativity. It's not until we start making decisions that limit the possibilities that art appears on the page. This is especially true of screenwriting, because the best scripts are often the ones that put less on the page. It is a process of reduction. Less is more.

So, please, stop writing that screenplay, or novel, or whatever it is - and start planning. Please focus on the story design first.

Commercial not Stupid

This book is about commercial storytelling, as opposed to the kind that you write for yourself, but is of little interest to anybody else. It presupposes that you want as large an audience as possible. Success demands an audience and that audience commands respect. Crafting a good movie pitch is story-selling at its core, so we are going to spend a lot of time looking at the pitch in particular. Moviemaking is a cut-throat business. The odds are against you. But you can improve your odds by applying the principles of this book.

But when we say 'commercial', we don't mean 'popular'. There are lots of stupid films that are lazy and unremarkable, yet extremely popular. We're not interested in that. Making films like these will pay the bills, for sure, but they aren't going to satisfy the soul. What we're looking for are stories that are both commercial AND thoughtful - meaningful stories with a social impact. And given that the development process can take years, why not spend the time crafting something of quality that you can be proud of and that audiences will keep coming back to time and time again?

This book is about creating stories that teach us something new - a transformational experience. We don't want the audience to come out the same way they went in. We want them to learn something about themselves and the world around them. And we want them to be entertained in the process. In other words, commercial. This means that the story must obey certain rules and expectations of the audience. If you are more interested in breaking boundaries - and less interested in maximising the number of people who will want to read, watch or listen to your story - then our advice is probably going to fall on deaf ears.

There are lots of books offering good advice on screenwriting. We're not trying to recreate the wheel here. But this book is different. Why? First of all, we are not academics. While we want to nurture your artistic voice, we also run a business. We want stories that sell. Not only do we develop new stories, but we take them to the markets, too. This means story-selling. It's an important learning experience that you won't get from development - and one that you are not likely to forget easily, either. Imagine spending years giving birth to your baby, only to have everyone tell you it's ugly, or that nobody cares. Dealing with sales agents, financiers, and distributors teaches you a lot about the demand side of the business and, more often than not, why they won't demand what you want to supply. We'd like to help you avoid some of potential pitfalls.

Many creative producers like to keep their writer close. They want to keep the writer focused and not to wander off-piste, as it were. If a writer disappears for a few weeks without a well-designed story, or ignores the story design altogether, then a producer is probably not going to like what they get back. Not necessarily because it's bad but because it's different. It wasn't the film that they wanted to make in the first place. And losing their support could kill the project.

We can't guarantee that you'll write a great work of art. That is your department. But what we can offer is a better way to get there in the first place.

PART THREE
STORYTELLING

What is a Story?

Good stories are good entertainment. We immerse ourselves in an unfamiliar world - full of interesting characters who face compelling challenges - and then we return back to our own, everyday lives once more. Good stories entertain us, but they are not told simply to entertain. Entertainment is the by-product of good craftsmanship. Instead, good stories educate. They enlighten. They elevate our consciousness. Perhaps that sounds pretentious? But it's true. Good stories return us to our lives different than before. They take us on a journey of self-discovery, as we vicariously live the lives of others.

For this reason, a story is not really about a series of events (fictional or otherwise). That is the narrative. Neither is a story about a particular person, or protagonist. That is a character in the narrative. Instead, a 'Story' is fundamentally a search for meaning. Stories teach us about ourselves and the human condition. Therefore, good stories have a purpose. They are transformational.

It is worth taking the time to reflect on the purpose of storytelling. The reason being that we have confused the meaning of the word 'Story' with the tools used to create one. By focusing on the tools, we lose sight of our goals. For example, a story is not the narrative. That is an expression of the story. And there may be many, valid expressions (aka narratives) for the same story. A story has to be 'about something'. But that 'something' is not a person, place, or period in time. Nor, is that 'something' about plot, action, conflict, genre, dialogue or a particular situation. These are tools of the trade - used to construct the narrative - but not the story itself. So what, then, is the 'Story'?

Good stories are fables. Bad stories lack conviction.

We are familiar with fairytales and fables. We remember them from our youth - read to us by our parents and care givers. They have overtly educational agendas. They do not hide their purpose. They are morality tales that impart folk wisdom. But all good, well-told stories have a similar objective. They have a point of view - a take on the world - that they want their audience to understand. They might take longer to unravel than a fable - and they might impart their point of view in a more subtle manner - but, to some degree, all good stories are fables at their core. The purpose of a good story is to teach us something. What is your fable?

If you do not have a fable, then you might have performance art. A lot of art house movies are like this - full of interesting atmosphere, character-studies, introspection and visual arts - but without an obvious purpose. The phrase, 'A slice of life' comes to mind. Commercial stories, on the other hand, are more explicit and obvious. They articulate a point of view and leave less to chance. They might leave some room for interpretation after they end but they still make a point about something without leaving their audience to wonder exactly what it is.

We want our audience to understand what our story is about. And, we want them transformed by the experience. It won't work if they are confused. The story must be made explicitly clear by the narrative.

Storytelling is a Ritual

The purpose of the storytelling ritual is to reinforce rules of conduct, propagate mythology, protect sacred knowledge, and to strengthen social bonds. In short, stories strengthen community by searching for shared meaning.

Commercial storytelling - the kind that has the broadest appeal and the most satisfying emotional outcome to the largest number of people - is an activity that re-affirms what the community already believes to be true. It does this by reconfirming what are perceived to be 'universal truths' - even if these are culturally specific. Often, stories will test and challenge the cultural norms and beliefs of the community before reconfirming them to be sacrosanct - as in the cautionary tale. Sometimes, they try to establish a new truth to replace an old one. But the most commercial stories do this in a way that doesn't confuse or confound its audience. People don't like to be told that they are wrong. They prefer to be told what they already want to hear. Otherwise, if the story does trounce on perceived truths, it must propose an optimistic alternative, so that the audience doesn't leave full of despair.

The storytelling ritual follows certain rules. Most narratives have a beginning, middle and end. There is conflict in the narrative. Characters are forced to confront crises in order to help them overcome their fears and achieve their goals. Thrillers, Film Noir, Romantic Comedy... all of these genres have certain structural expectations - similar to how different types of music have different rhythms, times, and scales. Audiences intuitively know all this from absorbing years of shared storytelling experience.

Given the above, a Story is not plot. It is not character, genre, dialogue, scenes, or situations. It is not action or conflict. These are all tools used to construct the narrative of a story but they are not what the story is about. This is an important difference between the approach to storytelling that we are advocating and all the other ones that you are likely to hear. We want you to get to the heart of what your story is really about before you even consider the narrative. This will ensure that your story is transformational by design and that it teaches us something new and noteworthy. If done correctly, then it has a much higher probability of success. It will effect more people emotionally and intellectually than the other stories that did not bother to do this.

The Story is a Debate

When we ask a writer to tell us what their story is about, nine times out of ten they will launch into a long description about their characters and what happens to them. This is not the story. This is the narrative. This is not what the story is about.

Instead, we want to know what we are going to learn from this story. What is it going to teach us about ourselves and the world we live in? Why is it relevant to us - or, indeed, anybody else who might pay to see it? Why does it need to be told right now? In other words, we want to know the purpose of the story.

A story is a debate about something important. This means that the storyteller must have something important to say. And they must say it with conviction. It helps to have some life experience to bear on a project. That doesn't mean you must only write about what you know. People often tell young writers to 'live a little' first, so that they can write from experience; write about what they know. This is very condescending. We are blessed with an imagination to overcome this obstacle. But a writer must write about something meaningful; something that they feel passionately about. There is no short-cut here.

A commercial story is likely to be about something meaningful to a lot of people. And a good story is likely to say something new, or at least explore something familiar in an novel way.

If you accept our definition of story, then your first job as a writer is to figure out the purpose of your story - what is the 'big idea'? What's it all about? What is the accepted truth that you are going to either challenge or confirm? In other words, what is the central idea of your story?

You begin with a statement of fact - either one that is universally accepted, or one that is highly provocative. Then you use narrative to debate that statement. In the end, you conclude your argument. If your narrative is well-constructed, then your audience is likely to agree with your conclusion - or at least find it a satisfying outcome. You, the writer, must have conviction about what the outcome should be. Then, you use your characters, scenes and plotting to debate your statement - ultimately, convincing the audience that the conclusion of the story - your conclusion - is the correct outcome.

Here's an example. One of your characters says up-front, "It is better to die on our feet than to live on our knees." This is perceived wisdom. We understand, then, that this is a story about the value of freedom and that it must never be compromised, or taken for granted. The audience expects this to be confirmed by the conclusion of the story.

Alternatively, the character could have said, "It is better to live a slave than never to have lived at all." This would be a more contentious statement. It is guaranteed to provoke a strong counter-response from the audience. But - if this is what the story is about - then it must be skilfully concluded to an emotionally satisfying outcome. Whichever position you take, you must convince the audience of the validity of your debate and the soundness of your conclusion. This takes conviction. Otherwise, you will convince no one.

A Commercial Story is a Debate with an Emotionally Satisfying Conclusion

To question the natural order of things is the remit of the storyteller. All of us at some point in our lives question the world around us - especially as children. We explore the boundaries of our understanding. As we grow older, we learn to frame our enquiry as a debate - one that hopefully leads to a well-argued and inevitable conclusion. This is what storytelling is all about: a debate around some central idea.

Well-crafted stories often postulate something provocative up front, debate the idea throughout the narrative, and then resolve the conflict in an emotionally satisfying way that either proves or disproves the idea put forth at the beginning. This is the standard modus operandi of debate. In other words, a story is about a central idea that creates conflict because it has at least two opposing sides that can be argued equally well. Like any good debate, a story begins with an introduction, provides evidence to support opposing points of view, and, ultimately, concludes on one side of the argument.

For example, the central idea of a story could be about how anyone can succeed when they believe in themselves and stick to their convictions. The narrative itself might set up the debate by creating circumstances in which this idea is severely tested. We might begin with a protagonist who has a dream or ambition but loses everything and everyone along the way. They are fired from their job. The bailiffs come knocking at their door. They are forsaken by friends and family. Yet, through sheer will-power, tenacity and fortitude, they embrace opportunity and ultimately achieve their goals. The story in this case is not about a particular character. It is about a perceived truth: that anyone who works hard enough will succeed. And the confirmation of that truth. It is emotionally satisfying because many people want to believe in it. The story in this case, then, is this: "You can be anything you want, so long as you want it badly enough."

You may have noticed that this story could have either a triumphant or tragic ending. I deliberately phrased it in this way. The reason being that we have not decided yet what the genre of this story should be - only that it debates a central idea and concludes that anything is possible once you set your mind to it. It is possible that the protagonist got what they wanted but that the sacrifice came at too high a price. Alternatively, they may be reunited and feted by all the loved ones who doubted them along the way and they all ride off into the sunset, happily ever after. The point I am trying to make is that the story is a debate around a central idea that comes to an emotionally satisfying conclusion. How the debate is structured is dependent upon many factors - such as genre. However, by knowing what your story is about at the outset, you can explore different forms of debate (Narrative) without losing sight of the story you want to tell.

You can probably see now that we see story design as a series of steps designed to bring the narrative into focus, little by little, until the end result feels like the best, most inescapable one. This is good story design and it should make writing a good story much easier to do.

Here are some examples of interesting stories based on universal truths or counter-truths that have absolutely no narrative structure yet:

"My story is about…"

- How love is dangerous; we often hurt the ones closest to us most of all.

- How we can change the world - not by gaining power and influence over others - but by changing ourselves and leading by example in our local community.

- How technology has brought us closer together but emotionally pushed us further apart; we are now more inter-connected but increasingly lonelier than ever before.

The Pitch is the Story Design

The rest of this book is going to focus on crafting a pitch. By 'pitch', we don't mean a one-sentence 'elevator pitch' as is often mentioned in screenwriting manuals. Instead, we have a very particular format for crafting a one-page pitch that is extremely useful in laying the foundation of a story. It tells all the stakeholders exactly what they need to know about the story and should enable them to make a decision on whether or not to move forward into further development.

We must give credit where credit is due. The basic anatomy of this pitch is something that we learnt from Alby James, a very talented creative producer and SEAM mentor. However, we have modified his format in a number of ways during our development process. Furthermore, we believe that there is an important distinction between story and narrative, which we will come to presently.

There are a number of benefits to writing a one-page pitch. First, it offers a great blueprint for writing a treatment and, eventually, drafting a screenplay. Second, it keeps everyone focused on the story, as opposed to the narrative, so that you might avoid development hell. Third, it's easier to bash out a bunch of one-pagers than it is to write a bunch of screenplays. This is particularly useful in Europe where there is practically no spec script market. It is our hope that writers can be more successful at getting commissions from well-constructed one-pagers. If so, it is a halfway-house between spec and commissioned scriptwriting that could benefit the industry as a whole.

PART FOUR
THE PITCH

Introduction to The Pitch

You've probably been to a movie where the characters and dialogue are witty, but nothing seems to be going anywhere. Even worse, the scenes gets longer and more self-indulgent, as if the writer was trying to amuse themselves more than the audience. You feel bored, agitated. You fidget. Your To-Do list pops into your head. Your mind wanders.

This happens when a storyteller writes without purpose. They don't know where they are going and neither does the audience.

When a storyteller writes with a purpose, they write with conviction. Every scene is committed to that purpose. The narrative has meaning. And the climax of the film is cathartic.

A writer must understand thoroughly what their story is about and what it is they want to say. Character, conflict, plot - these are all par for the course - but making adjustments to the narrative is simply rearranging the furniture. A solid foundation is required. As a storyteller, your first job is build that foundation and to be an architect. You can worry about the decor later. But the decor services the design. Once you know the story - the debate - then every element of your narrative, every character, every situation - is used to articulate the central idea towards a satisfying conclusion.

It is for this reason that we put so much emphasis on "The Pitch". It is a complete foundation of the story itself. You should be able to plug different characters and situations into it, as you search for the best way to fulfil its objectives. Otherwise, you'll need to start again from scratch.

Many people resist writing such a detailed pitch. They'd rather jump right in and begin a voyage of discovery by creating characters, composing scenes, and coming up with cool ideas. That may be so. There's nothing wrong with this approach at the outset. It can be a very effective way of freeing up your mind - a brainstorming exercise. But, at some point, you'd better sit down and write the pitch. If you don't, you'll be wasting your time and everyone else's. This is what makes the difference between a good script written in four months and one written in two years. If you have the income to spend several years writing one thing to the exclusion of all else, then good for you. Most of us do not have this luxury. And, so, we are better off constructing the pitch before we jump into the void.

Would you build a house without an architect? Would you jump right in and start constructing rooms, staircases, electrics, plumbing - with only a simple outline on a napkin? No, you would not. Why should it be any different with storytelling?

Brainstorming has its place. Keeping a journal, scribbling on index cards, saving the cat... these are all great methods to encourage free-form association. This book is not about that. You probably have your own, tried-and-tested methods of squeezing the juice from your brain. This book is about organising those ideas into a story, designed by default - not by accident. We want to make sure that the story is going to be meaningful and have a social impact - before we even begin outlining it.

The One-Pager Pitch

Most people think of a pitch as a couple of sentences. But, to us, that would be a teaser - something to hook our interest. The hard part is fleshing out the rest of it in order to create a blueprint for the story.

Writing a one-page pitch is not easy. It can drive you crazy. That's good. It's going to spare you that feeling several months down the line - when deadlines are looming and nothing seems to be working out the way you hoped it would. By focusing on design, you start to see where the problems are and it gives you time to fix them.

Let's think on how we might arrive at the heart of our story. We'll start with a familiar one. Take Romeo and Juliet. Everybody's familiar with the play. It's full of interesting characters, good dialogue, conflict and pathos. But we could tease it in a sentence: "Two teenage lovers pursue a love so profound that it defies even death itself." Notice that it does not contain any character names or plot detail, yet we already know a lot about this story. We can guess its genre, target audience and how it's going to end. It tells us a lot about the experience we're going to get.

But this isn't a pitch. It's a good start, certainly. But it's more like a logline - something the voiceover guy might say in the trailer. Or, a tagline - something you might see on a poster. Nevertheless, it's good to know. If you really don't have more than a minute in an elevator to sell your idea to an investor, then this hook might be all you need as your opening gambit.

Instead, we want a pitch to tell us everything we need to know in order to make an investment decision - bearing in mind that development is likely to occupy the next few years of our lives. Let's assume that you - the writer - have scheduled at least fifteen minutes with an executive to pitch your story. You need to be prepared to tell them everything they need to know to make a decision. And, if you do your homework, they should be able to make a decision on the spot. Otherwise, you're taking it to someone else.

The one-pager is short and simple but comprehensive. It tells us everything we need to know. We can invest in a one-pager. We don't need the script in front of us. That can come later.

Elements of The Pitch

Here is what we want to see in a one-page pitch - in this particular order:

Title
Genre
Dramatic Question
Premise
Tagline
Logline
Short Synopsis
Story Message

When a writer has assembled all the elements (above), then we have a story that we can get vested in (or not, as the case may be). Part of the reason why we feel this way is that it's very easy to get lost in the development process. It's easy to go astray when you don't really know where you're going. A good pitch tells you where you need to go. It gives you purpose. But it doesn't tell you exactly how to get there. That's what the Treatment is for.

If a writer cannot complete the pitch as described above, then they don't really have a story yet. They might have an interesting concept, some ideas about characters and scenes, etc - but they don't have a story. This is why the pitch is such a useful tool for weeding out the chaff. It is decisive. It tells you if there is a story or not.

You might be thinking that the pitch looks like a lot of work. Yes, it is. But it's time well spent. Consider this: the cheapest time to make the movie is scripting the movie. There are only a few people involved. You can chop and change scenes without giving the production a heart attack. Likewise, the cheapest time to script the movie is in the pitch. If you don't take the time to do so, you can easily get lost in development hell and lose the project altogether. And, don't forget, you can also keep the project but lose the freshness.

When there is heat on a project, everybody's excited. They want to see results. But if the project drags on for years, it starts to feel like yesterday's news. People will be more interested in the shiny new project that just walked in the door. It's human nature. It's unfortunate, but you can't avoid dealing with other people in this business. You must keep them engaged and then deliver on your promise. The pitch, then, is your promise - your blueprint. Whenever you go astray, just refer back to your pitch, and get yourself back on track.

As we said, the pitch is hard work. But what it really comes down to is this: a good pitch makes it easier to write a good Treatment; a good Treatment makes it easier to draft a good script. A good script makes it easier to package the elements you need to make a movie. And the more iterations you do on each, the cheaper and easier it is to deliver a great shooting script. It's simply a far more efficient way of working. And in this business, you can use all the help you can get.

If you are still sceptical, then you haven't been in a situation where you were well into drafting the script, when you realised that nothing seems to be working. The structure has gone awry, the characters aren't gelling and every change just seems to be making things worse. The project is unravelling. You've gone down too many dead-ends and you're getting close to burn-out. Even worse, the earlier drafts were far more satisfying than the current ones. What you've got on your hands is a dog's dinner.

We can't promise that a good pitch will save you from this experience - but you will certainly minimise the risk. Furthermore, when somebody else gives you notes - or an executive wants you to accommodate their 'great idea for a scene' - you can refer back to the pitch and see if that new idea really complements (or conflicts) with the essence of the story. You can ask the executive, "Does what you are suggesting service the story, or confuse it?" Every element of the narrative should, ideally, service the story - not confound it. Thinking in these terms will help you avoid a lot of those dead-ends and kill anything that's going to lead you on a fool's errand.

Your pitch will define the story development process. It is a blueprint for you and for any executives involved in the project. Given that the average script development process can take a long time, you need something to keep everybody on track. You need to stay focused. And that's what the pitch is for.

A Good Pitch is Good Story-Selling

The Pitch is the most important part of the storytelling process. Let us reiterate. There is nothing more important than a good pitch. Why? Because you have to be able to tell yourself and other people what your story is about. If you can't communicate your story, then you don't have a story - not one that other people will be interested in, anyway. You want to 'sell' the story to all the stakeholders involved, especially the audience. Put your sales cap on and work it.

If you are crap at pitching, that's fine. That's why we write it down as a one-pager. Then, you can practice and rehearse it to other people. Tell a friend what your story is about. Say it out loud to yourself. Listen to yourself falter, backtrack and dither. That's your problem - right there. You still don't know what your story is about. But don't worry, we're going to work on that.

The "One-page Pitch" should answer every conceivable and important question about your story. It is your story design document. And the first two elements of the pitch - Dramatic Question and Premise - answer the all important question, "What is the story about?" They create the critical debate that is the essence of your story - as expressed in your Story Message. After that, the other elements of the pitch define how you will construct your narrative in order to conclude the arguments central to that debate.

Step 1: Story Message - Pt 1

The first three steps of our story design process - **premise, dramatic question,** and **story message** - are going to work in harmony with one another and sum up the entire story. These are the 'Big Three' of story design and they will be the DNA of your story. Without them, you have no story. But, in order to get there, we are going to work our way backwards. By this, we mean that we must start with the message of the story.

Why do we start with the last item on our one-pager? Because it's the pay-off of the story. If we don't know the pay-off before we start, then we're writing without a purpose... which means the narrative will lack conviction... audiences will get bored and fidgety... and you will have wasted years of your life for nothing. When you ask people what they thought of your film, they will tell you the music was good (which means your movie sucked). People stop returning your calls. You become embittered. You get the idea. Don't write without a purpose. Start at the end. Start with the message of your story.

The Story Message concludes a debate

Every good story is a debate. It has arguments and counter-arguments that propel the audience towards a foregone conclusion. And since every story must be 'about something' - this is the time to figure out what the story is about.

We're going to begin by thinking about a topic or issue that we feel passionately about. It needs to be something that really gets our blood going; something that we can't wait to talk about, write about, pontificate about... for years to come (because it really might take years to get somewhere with it).

We won't worry about genre, or any other narrative elements at this point. All we want is to know how this story is going to end, because it is the conclusion of our story that will influence every other decision that we make. We do this in order to give our story a rock-solid foundation from which there can be multiple paths (and narratives). But all paths must lead back to the same conclusion.

Even though we will put the Story Message at the end of the one-pager, pitch document - we need to consider it now. All the elements of our pitch will gradually crystallise into a succinct statement of what the movie is about. The pitch will slowly bring the story into focus, line by line... leading the reader by the hand, step-by-step. When they get to the end of our one-pager pitch, they will reach your story message statement and understand precisely what the story is about. By which point, it will feel like a foregone conclusion. It should be a cathartic moment.

As we said at the outset, we will work backwards from the ending. This is because we want to determine the intellectual impact that the story will have on its audience. We will worry about the emotional impact later - in the narrative design. But, right now, we want to make sure that the story 'means something'. This will be an intellectual idea. Hopefully, it will be your, original idea. Then, you will craft the debate into your narrative and arrive at your conclusion (story message) in no uncertain terms.

Let's begin by thinking about a topical issue, or a compelling argument. It must be something we care about. Suppose you were conflicted by the recent wars in Afghanistan and Iraq. In particular, you were disturbed when Western governments enacted laws to permit the use of torture during interrogation. You might have strong views on whether or not torture is permissible. That's good. So do many other people. There are those who believe that the sacrifice of a single individual is justified if it saves the lives of many. Then, there are those who believe that torture is unacceptable in a free society, full stop - no matter what the perceived benefits might be.

You discuss the issue with friends and find that it's a polarising topic. Clearly, this will create a lot of conflict along the way, which will be good fuel for debate. You're off to a good start. However, you don't want to simply rehash a polemic in order to create controversy for controversy sake. You actually want to add something new to the debate; say something of significance that brings us to a new understanding of the situation.

You discover that - according to many researchers - torture is rarely effective, because it yields imperfect results. A strange relationship can develop between the victim and the torturer, which can lead to false evidence (WMD anyone?) And, frankly, people will say anything to avoid pain.

But what if there was a sure-fire way to get perfect results every time? What if we had new technology to help us get the answers we wanted - 100% guaranteed - but it resulted in the death of the victim? Under those circumstances, would this technique be justified? This would present an interesting twist on the debate. It would force the debate into two extremes and not allow anyone in the audience to sit on the fence. You file that away for later.

After ruminating on this issue for awhile, you decide to make the following argument: torture isn't justified - not because it's imperfect, or morally reprehensible in and of itself - but because it has terrible consequences. It opens the floodgates to far more reprehensible behaviour in future by setting a precedence for moral corruption. We govern ourselves with rules to ensure life, liberty and the pursuit of happiness for all. When we disobey our rules, we destroy everything worth fighting for. In other words, torture leads to moral corruption and the erosion of our society. Torture leads to tyranny.

What you come to realise is that the story message that matters to you is not whether or not torture itself is permissible but, rather, whether or not the ends justify the means. You cannot protect a cherished ideal by undermining it - even in the short-term. When someone is a hypocrite, other people cease to believe in their convictions - no matter how sincere they may be, or what the motivation behind their actions. If you want to defend a principle, then you cannot compromise it under any circumstances. When America - a country founded on freedom from persecution and the due process of law - made their citizens exempt from that due process, authorised illegal forms of torture at Guantanamo, and enacted the 'Patriot Act' in order to spy on their own citizens... they destroyed their credibility and undermined their moral authority. The 'War on Terror' was a war of ideologies. American won the fight but lost the war.

Now you have a strong conclusion. It doesn't have to be right or wrong. It is simply your personal conviction and your story must service your argument.

Your story will demonstrate that when we make exceptions to the rule, we compromise our principles and destroy ourselves. You can now write this story message in a couple of sentences. We don't have a title yet for our story, so we'll simply refer to it as the "dangerous precedence" story.

Unfortunately, if you were to lead the pitch with this conclusion - or any story for that matter - you're going to come across as preachy. This is why it's going to come at the end. It's inherently intellectual and not a great way to open. But it gives the story gravitas and meaning. This puts it way ahead of the pack. But it comes at the end.

We are going to bury our story message - like a dog buries a bone - in the narrative of our story. It's going to pop up in flashes throughout the elements of our pitch. We'll see hints of it here and there, but it won't fully surface until the end. Remember, it must be in the DNA. But when it comes, it's going to feel like a powerful closure.

In order to finesse our way towards the story message without coming across as didactic, we need to make the issue as personal and pressing as possible. What we have at the moment is something that is intellectually compelling but not emotionally compelling. Don't worry. We are going to connect to our audience through the narrative. The premise will make our story message relevant and the dramatic question will make it urgent. Our protagonist is going to live or die by it. The narrative will make it feel immediate and alive.

What the story is about > Explanation > Anecdote

Your story message is going to be a paragraph, or two. It will begin with a short sentence of what your story is about, followed by an explanation of that sentence. The final paragraph will be a personal anecdote as to why you want to tell this story.

In our "dangerous precedence" example, we have already worked out the explanation (that by destroying our principles - we destroy ourselves) and the personal anecdote (torture). What we don't have yet is a succinct, what-our-story-is-about sentence. We'll come back to that later - after we've worked out the premise and dramatic question.

The reason for including a personal anecdote in our story message is because we want our reader to understand our conviction and why they must care about this issue, too. Tell us why you - the writer - want to tell this story in the first place. What motivated you to come up with the original idea and tell this particular story at this particular point in time? Hopefully, it will explain why your story is topical and why other people should care about it. This is important, because other stakeholders who read your pitch will be wondering, "Why this story and why now?" This is an opportunity to make your case. You want to convince them that there is no better time for this story than the present, because it taps into a zeitgeist. And, if it doesn't, you can at least convince your reader that it's universal enough to appeal to anyone, at any time. At the very least, it gives you a chance to express your passion for the project - passion that is, hopefully, contagious.

For this reason, we like anecdotes. They personalise the writer's own journey and process of discovery. We are more likely to care about something you care about, plus it gives us insight into your personality and why we might want to spend the next few years with you in the sweatbox of development. We would encourage you, therefore, to think long and hard about why this story gets you excited. Try to explain that as best you can. It will help your reader project some of their own hopes and dreams onto your story project, too. No doubt, if you have a strong conviction about something, there must have been a reason for it. Write down this reason. Help the reader to empathise with you - the writer. They'll have a better understanding of where you're coming from and what you hope to achieve. Remember, you want to get them emotionally vested in your story. This is story-selling.

Does every story have to have a message? It should do. Otherwise, it serves no purpose other than to kill time. There are plenty of other ways to kill time. But spending millions of dollars to employ hundreds of people to realise a story on screen without a message is an incredible waste of resources - not to mention the waste of an opportunity. And our time is limited enough on this earth. For the time being, anyway. So, why not use that complex muscle between our ears to do something noble? Why not tell stories that mean something?

So, now we know what the message of our story... but we still can't answer the simple question, "What is the story about?" Don't worry. We're going to come to this in part two of the story message process. For now, we must put a pin in it and do some deep thinking on our premise and dramatic question. These two elements will give us what we need to come back and finish our story message.

Step 2: Premise

Now that you have found a story message that you think is personal and profound (and we say this without any irony whatsoever), you need to introduce it with a premise. Ideally, you want a pithy statment in the form of a 'universal truth'. This will help it resonate with a larger audience.

The Premise is an aphorism or proverb

There are many definitions of 'premise' in the storytelling world. For us, the premise is simply a perceived universal truth that will be tested in the narrative. Frequently, this will be a common aphorism, or proverb. It will determine the narrative structure and telegraphs the moral of the story. Great. Now, how do we get one?

Thankfully, literature is full of well-known premises. Here's a familiar one. "Absolute power corrupts absolutely." In fact, this seems like a really good premise for the "dangerous precedence" story example. You can imagine a narrative that tests the notion that the ends justify the means, ending in calamity. This, then, becomes the moral fabric of the story - the premise - and you have a pretty good idea how this fable is going to end. Most likely, the protagonist - or some other key character - is going to pursue power to the detriment of themselves and others. How exactly this will happen is not yet determined. But you know it's going to happen.

The Premise frames the debate

Many well-structured film scripts have a character introduce the premise within the first ten minutes of the film. Often, it's slipped in as cautionary dialogue. If it's done well, it feels natural and not like a giant neon sign flashing in the night. It foreshadows what is to come. In reality, it is framing the debate by establishing the premise of the story. Then, in the last ten minutes of the film, a character will summarise the story message. The premise and story message work together to frame and conclude your debate.

You might be wondering why we bother to have a single-sentence premise and a single-sentence concept at the beginning of our story message - isn't this a duplication of effort? Not necessarily. The premise is the universal truth that the audience is predisposed to believe in. Your story message - the one that tells us what the story is about - is your confirmation, or contradiction, of that universal truth. In other words, the personal voice that you have as an author comes through in your story message. You give the story meaning by either confirming or denying what the audience was predisposed to believe. Your story, then, becomes a journey of self-discovery for everyone involved.

For instance, you might not believe that "Absolute power corrupts absolutely". You might have an interesting story message that completely contradicts this premise. That is fine. You are going to test the premise in the narrative and prove it to be incorrect. The premise is simply a framing device. You let the audience know up front that this is what the debate will be about. Then, you prove, or disprove it in the end.

Working with our "dangerous precedent" example, we now have:

Premise: Absolute power corrupts absolutely
Story Message: When we compromise our principles, we destroy ourselves. Only by protecting our cherished beliefs, will we be triumphant. [Personal anecdote about torture laws during wartime].

You can see that we chose a story message that starts with something negative but ends on a positive. This is because we want to have an optimistic ending (more on that later). Otherwise, we will confirm the premise, but leave the audience in a state of despair. We'd like to avoid that if we can, because it's not good for business. Except in the rare occasion that we've written something so profound, so important and so necessary that it couldn't be told any other way. In that case, we hope it becomes a classic, and that nobody cares about how terrible it makes them feel afterwards - so long as they've had a revelation.

More Premise Examples:

An escape from reality leads to a day of reckoning
Love conquers all
The sins of the father are visited on the son
Blind trust leads to destruction

(For more Story Premises, check out: www.seam.tv/story-premise/)

Step 3: Dramatic Question

So far, you have created an intellectually compelling debate by determining your premise and story message. Now is the time to make it emotionally compelling by personalising the journey for the audience. We do this by coming up with a riveting dramatic question.

Our definition of a dramatic question is simple. It's a "What if...?" Sentence.

Here's an example: "What if we could live forever?" You can already see how this question will precipitate debate. Is it a good thing, or a bad thing? You can argue both in favour or against without having to commit yourself, leaving your audience in suspense until the end. In fact, whomever you ask this question to is likely to want to know your answer (as well as their own).

Good dramatic questions start the discourse but don't presuppose an obvious conclusion. The more provocative they are, the better. How about, "What if you were only given a week to live?" That's very provocative and very personal. Each of us might have very different ideas on what to do with our last week on earth.

It's important to bear in mind that we don't want to limit our options just yet by thinking about the narrative. For example, "What if human beings lost their humanity?" As erudite as this may sound, it's open-ended enough to invite lots of different narrative manifestations. One might be to look at a story during wartime, when decent people are driven to do unspeakable things with impunity. Or, you might take a completely different approach and craft a science fiction story where people are replaced by machines, or aliens, or taken over by a virus, or a drug (like Soma in Aldous Huxley's "Brave New

World") that results in the eradication of war and strife… but removes some of the more creative and passionate impulses. As you can see, this dramatic question opens up a debate about human nature and whether or not we can fashion a better (or worse) version of ourselves and our society. This is a good start.

The dramatic question personalises the story for the audience because they are forced to consider what they, themselves, would do in similar circumstances. You will often see the dramatic question put forth as the inciting incident in the first act of a drama. The protagonist is forced to consider something that will profoundly change their lives. If they choose to go forward, they can never go back and nothing will ever be the same again (remember the blue pill and the red pill in "The Matrix"?) This is what makes the story emotionally compelling.

The Dramatic Question provokes debate

Our point is that a well-fashioned, dramatic question provokes debate. And a debate invites conflict - the fuel of a good story. But the dramatic question doesn't presuppose any particular conclusion. It doesn't take sides. Instead, it opens up the floor to a process of discovery. For this reason, you might be tempted to begin the story design with a dramatic question. There's nothing wrong with this - so long as you know what your story message is. It might be a good thought exercise to come up with lots of different dramatic questions and then save them in a drawer somewhere, until you can arrive at a good story message that will complement one of them.

Here are some more dramatic questions to get you started:

What if women no longer needed to give birth?
What if you could take a pill to forget your past and start afresh?
What if sleep was no longer necessary?
What if your child, who you cherished above all else, was the devil?

For more dramatic questions, check out: http://www.seam.tv/seamteam/seamteam/story-concept-development/what-if/

Narrative-Free Storytelling

One of the great things about starting off with the Big Three - dramatic question, premise and story message - is that they don't presuppose any particular narrative, yet they can be quite fulfilling. The dramatic question and premise, in particular, can be recombined into different sets that presuppose very different outcomes. This is because the dramatic question is open-ended enough to stimulate debate, then the premise frames the debate, while the story message interprets the outcome. The conclusion is thus delivered in a way that is meaningful and relevant to the audience - and unique to the author.

For example, let's look again at the premise: "Absolute power corrupts absolutely." Right away, we know the moral of this story and have a pretty good idea how it's going to end. Most likely, the protagonist - or some other key character - is going to pursue power to the detriment of themselves. How exactly this will happen is not yet determined. But you know it's going to happen.

Now, let's try combining this "absolute power" premise with different dramatic questions and explore the outcome:

What if you could travel back in time? (Someone will use time travel for ill-gained power...and suffer the consequences)
What if you could read other people's minds? (Someone will use their power to manipulate others... and regret their powers)
What if you could punish the wicked? (Someone will assume power to seek justice... but their virtue becomes overwhelmed by their desire for revenge)

The premise and dramatic question are symbiotic. Together, they narrow down the universe to a finite set of story possibilities. The dramatic questions posed (above) offer both good and bad possibilities - but we determine which with our premise. Remember, a good premise tends to be based on a universal truth. A good story message either confirms this to be true, or challenges it by offering up a new truth in its place.

Hopefully, then, you can see the logical progression from story message, to premise, to dramatic question. We start with a compelling conclusion, tie it to a universal truth, then personalise it with an emotionally compelling question.

Putting it all together

Returning to our "dangerous precedence" example, let's choose a dramatic question that we believe will make our story more emotionally compelling:

Dramatic Question: What if we had the power to extract people's memories in the interest of national security?

Premise: Absolute power corrupts absolutely

Story Message: When we compromise our principles and take away our civil liberties, we destroy ourselves. Only by protecting our cherished beliefs will we be triumphant. [Personal anecdote about torture laws during wartime].

Extended Example...

One of us worked on a project with a character who had a very dark past but who was trying to put it behind them and become a better person. The project was inspired by an article in which a WWII nazi commander was finally apprehended after a sixty-year man hunt. When they took him into custody, the community in which he had lived for many years were shocked to learn the truth of his identity. He had always been a model citizen who had gone out of his way to help others. He had been a pillar of the community. He died in jail.

Many would call this justice, because there is a belief that a person can never truly atone for atrocious crimes. It triggered a debate about whether or not a bad person could ever become good? What if you had done something in your past that you were ashamed of and learnt the humility to want to set things right? What if you spent every day of your life working to erase that shame? Could you ever find redemption in the eyes of others? Would you be open about your past - or hide it away forever? Would your friends and family ever forgive you, if they knew the truth? Would your community learn to accept you for who you are now - rather than for who you were then?

These were powerful questions that we discussed in a workshop. We began to debate a familiar question - can a person every really change themselves fundamentally, or do they remain the same despite their circumstances? We wondered if getting a second chance in life would precipitate change, or if you had to have goodness somewhere inside you from the start - even if you did terrible things later - in order to rediscover it again? We debated the nature of good and evil. We all know how good people can be put into morally corrosive situations. And we figured that the desire to have a second chance in life was a pretty universal aspiration - that, at some point in our lives, all of us wish we could go back and fix our mistakes, erase our embarrassing moments in the past, and craft a better version of ourselves.

In the end, we found our conclusion: the truth will set you free. No matter what you do to hide your horrible past, it will catch up to you. You are better off coming clean and finding redemption by helping others to resist the pressure to do wrong - even if there is a gun to their heads - because you know, better than anyone, the nature of evil.

Here, then, are the Big Three that can be used to tell a story that frames the issues debated (above):
- Dramatic Question: "What if you could escape your shameful past by assuming a new identity?"
- Story Premise: "Evil flourishes when a good man does nothing."
- Story Message: Hiding the truth may give you a second chance in life but you will ultimately fail, because only the truth will set you free. (Followed by our anecdote about the origin of the story).

You can understand our story with the Big Three without knowing anything about our characters, genre, setting, etc. You know that the story will reconfirm a universal truth - "Evil flourishes when a good man does nothing" - and that it will challenge this idea by allowing someone to live a lie in order to find their freedom in order to do good. But that this lie will somehow put them or their community in jeopardy. They will be forced to choose between revealing the truth or letting something horrible happen - and that their new identity is a form of self-denial, preventing them from actualising their dreams, unless they are prepared to come clean and avert tragedy.

This is more art than a science but here is how we might come up with the Big Three for, 'The Godfather":

- Dramatic Question: "What if you wanted to leave the powerful crime family that you were born into but realised that you were the only one who could save them from annihilation?"
- Story Premise: "Blood is thicker than water."
- Story Message: This is a story about how family values can be perverted by power and kill the family they are meant to protect. When obsession with a family's honour and security precludes love and kinship, the family is destroyed. When filial piety becomes absolute, self-serving, and audacious - it destroys the object of its loyalty and affection.

(To see some more dramatic questions, or to share some of your own, check out: http://www.seam.tv/seamteam/seamteam/story-concept-development/what-if/)

Step 4: Story Message - Pt 2

Give yourself a pat on the back, because you've done most of the heavy-lifting. From here on in, composing the narrative should be downhill racing. However, we can't traipse off to the next step just yet. We need our story message to answer the simple question, "What is this story about?"

If you recall our discussion in the chapter about commercial storytelling, we used simple phrases to describe what our story was about. Here they are again:

"My story is about…"
- How love is dangerous; we often hurt the ones closest to us most of all.
- How we can change the world - not by gaining power and influence over others - but by changing ourselves and leading by example in our local community.
- How technology has brought us closer together but emotionally pushed us further apart; we are now more inter-connected but increasingly lonelier than ever before.

This is what we want for the first line of our story message - something simple and profound - that we can relate to in a single sentence. After which, we can give more explanation and follow-up with our anecdote.

Going back to our "dangerous precedence" story, we know that our story deals with an abuse of power. Given our interest in the government's justification of extraordinary measures in extraordinary times in an effort to preserve our safety, we came to the realisation that the ends don't justify the means, because of the damage they do to our principles. There is an inherent irony in this. When our lives are threatened, we often end up taking away the very freedom that makes life worth living (and dying) for.

Here, then, is how we might put this together in our example:

Dramatic Question: What if the government was able to read our minds and extract our secrets in the name of national security?

Premise: Absolute power corrupts absolutely.

Story Message: This story is about how the ends do not justify the means and that the first casualty of war is our own freedom, despite the fact that we fight to protect our liberty. When we compromise our principles by invading our privacy, we destroy ourselves. Only by protecting our cherished beliefs, will we be triumphant.

During wartime, governments enact laws that eliminate civil liberties, remove due process of law and justify the torture of our enemies and, sometimes, even our own citizens. Their justification is that extraordinary times demand extraordinary measures. Personally, I was horrified by what was allowed at Guantanamo - not because I find torture inherently evil, if it can save the lives of many - but, rather, that it sets a dangerous precedence in motion from which we can never recover. By undermining our moral authority and eroding our ideals, we do irreparable harm to our society and, ultimately, to ourselves. Our ideals are not principles of convenience - to be chopped and changed when they prove inconvenient. They must be upheld, especially when tested. We fight to preserve them every day of our lives. Why, then, do we rush to destroy them and everything worth fighting for, when we feel ourselves under threat? No, we must adhere to our principles - maintain a higher moral purpose - or, suffer the consequences.

Hopefully, it has become obvious by now that the 'Story Message' is where you actually answer the question, "What is the story about?" When someone picks up your one-pager, they will be lead by the hand, step-by-step towards your story message. They will explore the dramatic question, premise, genre, tagline, logline and synopsis… in that sequence. During the course of this process, the story will come together in their mind. You are helping them realise the same inevitable conclusion that you did - so that they will find your conclusion difficult to argue against. By the time they reach the end of the page, they not only know what the story is about but you have lead them through a process of discovery. Now they know your story and they begin to perceive it as their own.

At this point, you will notice that we have a pretty good outline of our story - all without adding any characters, genre or plotting. Nevertheless, we have a story that is going to be topical, compelling, and meaningful. The point we want to make is that a story is not the narrative. We have crafted our "dangerous precedence" story without needing any narrative whatsoever.

Now that we have an skeleton of the story, let's go and put some meat on the bones.

Step 5: Genre

A sales agent once told us about a hot property they'd acquired. They described it thus: "Werewolves in space! Where the moon is always full! Need I say more?" Well, actually, yes. First of all, we know nothing about the story itself, so we have no idea what this film is about. Second, we can assume there's going to be blood and guts...but is this a horror film, or a comedy? I could easily be either - or, both. Is it something along the lines of "An American Werewolf in London", or "Alien"? The audience isn't necessarily the same.

The "Big Three" tell the story, while the Genre sells the story

There is a complicity between the audience and the storyteller when it comes to genre. Every genre has certain conventions which the audience instinctively knows and expects to be obeyed - even if they are unable to articulate precisely what those conventions are. If not, the story sows confusion. Confusion is bad for business.

For instance, everyone knows what is supposed to happen in a romantic comedy: the principal characters hate each other in the beginning but ultimately, fall in love. The pleasure comes from seeing how they come together. And the more impossible the obstacles standing between them, the more satisfying the conclusion - because "Love conquers all." But genre doesn't inform the story - only the narrative. Again, we're sticking to our guns here: the story is independent of the genre.

So, we can establish that genre informs the narrative structure. We know that with each genre come certain expectations of the narrative. But the allows the genre to be used to pre-sell the story to a potential audience. Genre telegraphs the emotional experience and helps the audience to self-select. People look at the poster and know - at a glance - what kind of story experience they're likely to get. They know if it's targeting them, personally, and whether or not the elements (talent or material) is going to heighten their enjoyment of it. Film trailers do their best to highlight all the conventions of the genre in two minutes, so that there is no confusion in anyone's mind what to expect - "This is what you're going to get... and more!" At the very least, the film should meet the expectations set by its marketing. Hopefully, it will exceed them. Otherwise, people are going to be disappointed. It's not far off from choosing a holiday destination based on a glossy brochure, only to find that what you get is nothing like what was promised by the photographs. That's a promise that failed to deliver.

Familiar... but different

Genre, then, is a promise of what's to come - which makes it a very convenient marketing tool. Genre can communicate a lot about a project in as short a time as possible to a population that is self-absorbed and distracted by the noise of everyday life. It helps to inform a purchasing decision. And film marketing people love it for this very reason.

The trick for the writer is, of course, to give the audience something familiar - but different. The audience is coming to see their work based on a promise. That means it must follow convention. Not slavishly. It is fresh and exciting when the boundaries are explored and tested - but ignore them at your peril. If you are sold a romantic comedy and it ends up being a melodrama about a terminally ill cancer patient - you're not going to be happy about it. Of course, it could be a very good movie at the end of the day - but it didn't set the right expectation. You were duped. Remember the holiday brochure? If we knew the beaches were going to be clogged with touts, lager louts, rude waiters and angry children... we would have chosen a different time of year to go. Or, not gone at all, as the case might be.

Films as Widgets

Film financiers, sales agents, and distributors love genre, because it tells them something about the demographic of the audience they will be selling to and the potential market size. It helps them create financial projections by ignoring the artistic aspects of a film project and reducing it to a widget. Genre is a form of 'widgetisation'. It allows them to identify similar movies from the past to use in their spreadsheet analysis - e.g. "Running the Comps."

Given the above, you - the writer - want to give these people a widget, so they can understand what kind of a film this is going to be, how they are going to market it and to whom. Ideally, this would be THEIR job. But you'll find that many people in the business-end of film business don't like things out of the ordinary. They don't want a "Sci-fi/Musical/Horror" to take to market, or run financial projections on. Never mind that the "Rocky Horror Picture Show" was one of the most successful cult films of all time... they aren't interested in outliers. They want widgets. They want things to be easy. So, make it easy.

This means that you should pick your genre wisely. Try to pick ONE genre to describe your narrative. If you think a hybrid would be more accurate (e.g. "Comedy Horror"), then go ahead but be judicious. The more hybrid and hyphenated a project, the harder it will be to sell. The more unusual the hybrid, the fewer 'comps' sales agents have to run. Consider whether you really need that hybrid. Your horror story might have lots of comedy in it but that doesn't change the fact that it's predominantly a horror movie. A comedy can have tragic moments but it doesn't necessarily make them it a 'Tragi-Comedy', either.

We say this based on experience. Some of us learnt the hard way. For example, here at SEAM we love a good comedy-thriller, or sci-fi/film noir - such as "Dr. Strangelove" and "Blade Runner", respectively. But if these films were pitched to the public this way - or, even, to the film financiers - they would go over like a lead balloon. Comedy-thrillers are an interesting example of this. They happen to be our favourite type of narrative style but they are few and far between. Nobody knows what a comedy-thriller is. People always ask us for examples. Therefore, it's best to steer clear of that one. Better to call it a 'thriller'. The fact that it has comedic moments... well, that's a bonus. If it has lots of action and epic set-pieces... then, better yet, call it action-adventure (that's going to sell better). Keep it simple. Keep it familiar.

That said, there is a danger that a hybrid will fall between two stools in the final product. By not truly committing to one genre or another, a hybrid could fall flat. One of our producers was involved with a film that tried to be a gangster-melodrama but it was marketed to teens as an gangster movie. When the predominantly youth audience showed up to watch an urban gangster picture, they saw a 'worthy' and 'earnest' story about a man grappling with the failure of his marriage. Needless to say, they were totally confused - and they panned it… on their mobile phones during the opening weekend. Ouch! Likewise, a more mature audience - who might have appreciated this narrative more - was turned off by the gangster youth marketing and didn't go to see it.

A hybrid genre should be equal to more than the sum of its parts. Conversely, calling something a 'drama' is the kiss of death. It means there is no genre and it's going to be a really tough sell. The campaign will end up focusing on the talent's track record, because there's nothing else to go on: "From the director of… the creators of… based on a re-imagining of a true story…"

If you really want to write a kitchen-sink, slice-of-life story - that's fine. But first ask yourself whether or not you could make it a genre-driven narrative. For example, we've seen some interesting dramas that could easily have been thrillers, mysteries, or police-procedurals. If they had been, they would have been appreciated by more people - without losing sight of the underlying story. It's worth considering.

Let's look at another example before we go back to our "dangerous precedence" story. Imagine that you have a dramatic question like this, "What if your parents turned out to be aliens?" And your premise is, "The sins of the father are visited on the son." By locking in the genre, we limit the possibilities of the narrative. If the genre was action-adventure, then the narrative might be that the protagonist finds out that they are an alien, too - perhaps with superpowers - and it's up to them to save mankind. Alternatively, if the genre was a comedy, the protagonist might be forced to come to terms with their own alien transformation during puberty on prom night. Or, if it was a thriller, the protagonist comes to realise that they are being hunted down by a secret intelligence agency, because they are the progeny of an alien that escaped their custody from Area 51. The point we are making is that genre will determine narrative structure and helps us bring everything into focus.

There are lots of genres, sub-genres and hybrid genres to choose from. Be judicious and try as best you can to stick to one. But, also, try to make each hybrid genre more than the sum of its parts. For some reason, we've come across a number of romantic comedies lately in which the protagonist is dying of a chronic disease. This sends mixed messages, often falling between two stools. As an audience member, I know what to expect of a romantic comedy. But what am I supposed to make of a scenario where: boy meets girl, loses girl, gets her back again, just before she dies of cancer? We're not saying this cannot be a great story but it's a tough sell. Might it not be better pitched as a tragedy? For example, the tragic love story, "Love Story", starring Ali MacGraw and Ryan O'Neal, was a hugely popular film in its day; a real tear-jerker that sold itself as such and didn't disappoint. It had a message like this: "True Love is an experience worth having, even if it doesn't last forever." That's a tragic love story.

Going back to our "dangerous precedence" example, we might decide to choose science-fiction as the genre. This way, we can explore how a new technology forces radical social changes that could end in dystopia if it goes unchecked. Or, if we decide that harmony must be restored, we can decide to make the story a thriller. Even though it has some elements of sci-fi, we might prefer to structure the narrative in such a way as to have an innocent protagonist caught up in a conspiracy and it's up to them to figure out what's going on and restore harmony, before they run out of time.

Genre sets expectations. You must meet or exceed them to be commercially successful. Therefore, pick one genre that helps sell your story.

Step 6: Tagline & Title

"In space, no one can here you scream." Isn't that great? You can see it on the poster and you know right away that it's a horror film with sci-fi elements ("Alien"). Taglines are teasers - short, single sentences that help to sell the project. It's worth taking the time to craft a good one.

You often see taglines used as branding for products and services around the world: "Think Different" (Apple), "We try harder" (Avis), "Empowering the Internet generation" (Cisco). Think of the tagline as branding for your creative work. What's the message that you want the audience to take away from your story? Hopefully, your tagline will be something that reinforces the genre and teases them to want to know more about what you're offering.

The Tagline confirms the Genre

You want to find something suitable, creative and memorable. You want it to be catchy. You want it to go viral. This is the job of the film marketing department, we know, but let's help them out a little because they are time-pressured and distracted, especially when they've got thirty other pictures to market besides your own. You're going to make your pitch POP from the pile with a catchy tagline. You are going to be your own marketing department.

You've probably noticed by now that both genre and the tagline are part of selling your story. Think of it as putting together a sales package. You want to make your pitch irresistible to the business dev people.

Here are a few taglines for inspiration:

"All the power on earth cannot change destiny." (Godfather 3)

"Letting go of your past is hard... especially when it's dating your mom." (Mr Woodcock)

"After a night they can't remember comes a day they'll never forget" (Dude, Where's My Car?)

"Family isn't a word. It's a sentence." (The Royal Tenenbaums)

"A story of a man who was too proud to run!" (High Noon)

"The biggest risk in life is not taking one." (Proof)

"One hit could ruin your whole day." (Pineapple Express)

"History is made by those who break the rules." (Men of Honour)

"Trapped in time. Surrounded by evil. Low on gas." (Army of Darkness)

"Protecting the Earth from the scum of the universe." (Men in Black)

"A lot can happen in the middle of nowhere." (Fargo)

"There is no gene for the human spirit." (Gattaca)

"The first casualty of war is innocence." (Platoon)

"Reality is a thing of the past." (The Matrix)

"If at first you don't succeed, lower your standards." (Tommy Boy)

"Fifty million people watching but no one saw a thing." (Quiz Show)

"The hanging was the best show in town but they made two mistakes: They hung the wrong man and they didn't finish the job." (Hang 'Em High)

The Title relates to the Tagline

Now is a good time to consider your title. Now that you've worked your way through the story and the narrative genre, you want to capture the essence of your story in the title. Imagine your story as a beautifully wrapped present. Now, you want to put a bow on it.

Oftentimes, the title and tagline complement one another. This makes them a good couplet to consider in a single pass. Titles often telegraph the emotional experience by using a character name (Indie film or biopic), familiar phrase used in a quirky way (action or comedy), or a tough sound bite (action). Choose your title carefully and don't use something that's throwaway. It'll stick forever.

Here are some tagline & title combinations that resonate together:

"Death doesn't take no for an answer" (Final Destination)

"They took everything he had... except his rage." (Collateral Damage)

"The longer you wait the harder it gets." (The 40-Year-Old Virgin)

"He doesn't care if you're naughty or nice." (Bad Santa)

"Earth. It was fun while it lasted." (Armageddon)
"For Harry and Lloyd, ever day is a no-brainer." (Dumb and Dumber)
"Even a hit man deserves a second shot." (Grosse Pointe Blank)
"The thing that won't die in the nightmare that won't end" (The Terminator)

Going back to our "dangerous precedence" example, we might flesh it out like so:

Title: Memory Serves
Genre: Thriller
Dramatic Question: What if the government was able to invade our minds and extract our secrets in the name of national security?
Premise: Absolute power corrupts absolutely.
Tagline: Winning hearts and minds… one mind at a time.
Story Message: This story is about how the ends do not justify the means and that the first casualty of war is our own freedom, despite the fact that we fight to protect our liberty. When we compromise our principles by abolishing privacy, we destroy ourselves. Only by protecting our cherished beliefs, will we be triumphant. [personal anecdote].

Step 7: Logline

So far, you've completed the first five steps towards a very comprehensive story without making any decisions yet on what characters or plot will be used to tell the story. Now is the time. And the logline is the place to narrow down the universe of possibilities to determine the main agents of change. Who will be the ones to create the conflict and find the resolution?

The Logline identifies the agents of change

Good stories are full of memorable characters. Coming up with great characters is essential to good storytelling. However, you have done a great deal of work already to narrow down your character universe through the previous five steps. You probably have a much clearer idea now as to what type of characters you will need in your narrative to tell the story that you want to tell.

A good logline will introduce the main agent(s) of change. Often, this will be the protagonist and antagonist, but not always. The main agent of change could be a tsunami that alters the course of many people's lives in an ensemble piece. Your logline is going to tell us who, how and why. But you're not going to tell us the whole story here. Leave that for the short synopsis. Instead, you're going to tease a little more. You're going to set up the narrative without concluding it. You might even leave the logline on a cliff-hanger in order to get the reader to keep reading to the end of your pitch. In fact, I would advise you to reveal the first major turning point - the inciting incident - and leave the reader wondering how in the world the conflict that you create is ever going to be resolved.

It is important to keep the number of characters - or, agents of change - to a minimum. As soon as you introduce a bunch of names, the brain has to perform a lot of calculus in a short amount of time to keep them all separate and defined. You - the writer - may have lived with these characters for a long time, so you know them by heart. But please pity the reader who does not. All they see are names on a page. It doesn't mean much to them - yet. Therefore, you'll want to use a few names at most. Anything more is confusing. Remember, confusion is bad for business.

Let's go back to our "dangerous precedence" story, which we've now titled, "Memory Serves":

Title: Memory Serves
Genre: Thriller
Dramatic Question: What if the government was able to invade our minds and extract our secrets in the name of national security?
Premise: Absolute power corrupts absolutely.
Tagline: Winning hearts and minds… one mind at a time.
Logline: When an experimental memory extraction process proves a success, intelligence officer Chris Stevens (35) authorises its use on a high-profile terrorist suspect involved in an imminent plot against a major US city. Unfortunately, the memories can only be 'read' by implanting them in someone else, preferably with a close DNA match. With time running out, Stevens authorises the kidnap of the suspect's sister, Maria (23), and uses her to test the memory transfer and uncover the plot. The transfer is successful, but not without psychotic side-effects that grow worse by the hour. Forced to trace the steps where her new memories lead her, Maria must penetrate the terrorist ring and risk her life before possibly losing her mind.
Story Message: This story is about how the ends do not justify the means and that the first casualty of war is our own freedom, despite the fact that we fight to protect our liberty. When we compromise our principles by abolishing our privacy, we destroy ourselves. Only by protecting our cherished beliefs, will we be triumphant. [personal anecdote].

Step 8: Short Synopsis

Now you are ready for the narrative. You want to pull all the elements together and bring the story to a satisfying conclusion. The short synopsis is what it says it is - 'short' and a 'synopsis' of the narrative. What this means is that you are going to tell the whole story in a couple of paragraphs. And, when you do, you're going to showcase exactly how the Premise and the Dramatic Question frames the debate, while adhering to the guidelines of the Genre and fulfilling the promise of the Tagline. In other words, the short synopsis outlines the main beats and turning points of the narrative. Hopefully, it will demonstrate that the story is a well-structured argument that follows the expectations of the genre, while coming to a satisfying conclusion.

The Short Synopsis structures the narrative

If your narrative is going to adhere to a three-act structure, then we would advise you to make the key turning points very explicit. In other words, here are some of the beats you want to make clear in your short synopsis:

First paragraph: Set-up and Inciting Incident
Second paragraph: First Act Climax, Midpoint and Second Act Climax
Third paragraph: Third Act Climax and Resolution

Hopefully, it is clear to you now why we have the Logline and Short Synopsis when they seem to repeat similar information. The Logline gives you an opportunity to introduce your main agents of change, followed by the reveal of the Inciting Incident. Now, you give the reader a moment to digest the ramifications of the conflict that you have set-up and who some of the principal characters are - so that when they see their names again, they feel familiar to them. In the Short Synopsis, we deepen the engagement between the reader and the conflict by laying out the structure of the narrative and, hopefully, demonstrating how the story will have a satisfying outcome.

After considering the above, let's look at what the one-pager might look like for, "Memory Serves", including a short synopsis:

Title: Memory Serves

Genre: Thriller

Dramatic Question: What if the government was able to invade our minds and extract our secrets in the name of national security?

Premise: Absolute power corrupts absolutely

Tagline: Winning hearts and minds… one mind at a time.

Logline: When an experimental memory extraction process proves a success, intelligence officer Chris Stevens (35) authorises its use on a high-profile terrorist suspect involved in an imminent plot against a major US city. Unfortunately, the memories can only be 'read' by implanting them in someone else, preferably with a close DNA match. With time running out, Stevens authorises the kidnap of the suspect's sister, Maria (23), and uses her to test the memory transfer and uncover the plot. The transfer is successful, but not without psychotic side-effects that grow worse by the hour. Forced to trace the steps where her new memories lead her, Maria must penetrate the terrorist ring and risk her life before possibly losing her mind.

Short Synopsis: Maria, a first generation American, works diligently as a nurse at a local hospital, until she is kidnapped by a black-ops division of Homeland Security, and charged with treason. Duty officer, Stevens, accuses her of being a deep-cover, 'sleeper' agent, brainwashed to forget her training, until she is activated by her handlers. Too terrified to argue, she agrees to take a 'truth serum' under interrogation to prove her innocence. But, soon after, she remembers things that she can't deny are incriminating. Worried there may be truth in the allegations, Maria agrees to cooperate and follow the lead to wherever her new memories take her, and into the heart of the terrorist cell.
Facing danger and her own mental deterioration, Maria becomes convinced that she's somehow involved in a plot to destroy Washington D.C.

Only when she sees a memory of herself in the mirror, does she realise that her memories are not her own - but her brother's. Stevens admits to using a form of DNA replacement therapy to meld her brother's memories with hers. If she can uncover the plot in time, she has a shot at saving his life - and her own. Spurred on by a belief that her brother was an innocent caught up in something he was coerced into, Maria agrees to push on - despite the consequences - in the hope of absolving her brother.

In the end, Maria gets the proof she needs and stops the plot. Back at Stevens' facility, however, she learns that there is no way to reverse her condition. Even worse, her brother is dead. The memory extraction technique was invasive. His brain was shredded in the process and, now, Maria's memories are all that is left of him. Angry and confused, Maria uses her new-found skills to break free of her captors and confronts Stevens. He tells her that extraordinary times demand extraordinary measures. It is his hope that the DNA replacement therapy that was used to infect Maria can someday be perfected as a pre-emptive strike without the need for military engagement. If so, wars can be won by changing hearts and minds - quite literally from the inside - by brainwashing combatants. He entreats her to cooperate and justifies the sacrifice she has made for her adopted country. She has already survived longer than expected and her condition will yield important scientific insights. She must understand the bigger picture, here. Maria considers what Stevens is saying, before strapping him to the memory extraction unit. It's going to get crowded, she knows, but with Steven's memories in her head, too, she just might get a shot at bringing down the people he works for and stop their plan from ever coming to fruition.

Story Message: This story is about how the ends do not justify the means and that the first casualty of war is our own freedom, despite the fact that we fight to protect our liberty. When we compromise our principles and abolish our privacy, we destroy ourselves. Only by protecting our cherished beliefs will we be triumphant. [personal anecdote].

PART FIVE
WHAT NEXT?

The Short and Long of It

If you write a cracking one-pager, it should be easier for someone to commission you to write the script. By writing many one-pagers, you can pitch a lot of projects without having to write as many spec scripts. Nevertheless, those pitches have enough detail to enable you to hit the ground running, should you be commissioned to write a screenplay. Whatever happens, you should plan to write both a short and long treatment as your next steps to any project.

You might not be asked to write a Treatment before delivering a draft but you should do so anyway. It will help you write fast and efficiently when it comes time to draft the script. Also, it demonstrates to your commissioner that you are sticking to the same story and helps them arrive at the same decisions that you do. I like Short Treatments to be around 4-6 pages. They flesh out the main turning points of the story by providing greater detail in the narrative. Ideally, you could fit one act per page.

A long treatment goes even further by beating out each individual scene. Given that there are roughly 40 scenes in most commercial movies, you're looking at a document close to twenty pages. Nevertheless, by the time you have finished all this work, you have a much easier time drafting the first draft of your script. You'll know exactly what scenes to write, what needs to happen in each of those scenes and that your narrative will be well-structured.

An Optimistic Ending

It's worth bearing in mind that commercial stories often have optimistic endings. This is not the same as saying a 'happy ending'. For example, the ending of the movie, "Wall Street", directed by Oliver Stone, does not have a happy ending. Our protagonist is going to jail for a crime that he did commit. Nevertheless, it is an optimistic ending, because the protagonist goes willingly, knowing that he must be punished for his crime. But, he has a future worth looking forward to. He's made peace with his father and we believe that his girlfriend will wait for him. This is an ending full of 'hope' for the future. That's an optimistic ending. It's emotionally satisfying, because the bad are punished. And a good man who has done wrong has learnt a valuable lesson - and will be a better man for it.

Tragedies don't end happily but the protagonist usually comes to a moment of self-realisation before their fall. Think on Faustus. He knew what he was getting into, but felt that he could avoid (or damn) the consequences. He is aware that his misfortune is entirely of his own making. He doesn't go willingly, but he acknowledges his fate. Justice is served and the world can return to its prior equilibrium. The audience has learnt a valuable lesson from his misfortune and it's an optimistic ending because it portends hope for the rest of mankind - that we can learn from the mistakes of others and avoid them.

You may also remember my rumination on the nineteen-seventies film, "Love Story", in the Genre chapter. Given that the message could be: "Better to have loved and lost than never to have loved at all" - we can confirm that this has an optimistic ending, even if it's an incredibly sad one. Suffice to say, then, that a commercial ending should be optimistic. It's not impossible to end on a down note but nihilistic endings are not going to be as commercially successful. If the Ryan O'Neil character in "Love Story" had turned into a miserable bastard, as a consequence of losing the love of his life, we'd be left with a pretty empty experience. It would encourage us to avoid complicated relationships - not a life-lesson that we yearn for as an audience.

SEAM Storyselling

If you would like to discuss what you've read in this book with other writers producers and creative consumers - then join our Story Design Group at "**Shared Experience Art Machine**" - (www.seam.tv/groups/story-design) The Group is open to any interested parties and includes further examples and expands on some of the ideas expressed in this book.

Shared Experience Art Machine is a community for artists and their audiences to come together to create meaningful entertainment with a social impact. We invite both professionals and emerging artists to explore innovative storytelling methods and to collaborate on experimental projects.

At SEAM we are designing a project workshop that we call, "Perfect Pitch". It is a collaborative environment where storytellers are free to work together in order to develop story ideas that they can then advance individually. Certain elements of the pitch are brainstormed collectively and tested on the SEAM community. When a writer has a story idea, they use our website to create their own story design document, a one-pager pitch. This pitch is then market tested with the public and voted upon by our community. Winning pitches are circulated to established producers production companies and distributors.

The purpose of the "Perfect Pitch" project is to help writers hone their craft and encourage them to discover other partners to work with on future projects. Over the years, we have found that writing is enhanced by constructive collaboration. Let's be honest, writing is a lonely business. But when you have a trusted community of peers and mentors with whom to discuss your projects and other writers with whom you can collaborate, the results are superior. Furthermore, we aim to improve the quality of development and the commercial success of projects by engaging the public. Our system is designed to address the structural flaws within the entertainment industry - namely, that writers and producers pitch stories to distributors, rather than to the public. This is inefficient because the distributor is not the end customer and has a conflict of interest. The distributor prefers something identical to what they sold successfully before, whereas the audience is looking for something new - "familiar but different".

We believe that by establishing in advance that there is an audience for a project, we can surmount some of the financing obstacles that plague our business. This necessitates finding a way to gauge audience approval and sound metrics that will convince financiers that a project can be commercial - without relying on the personal opinion of distributors. Film history is full of highly profitable movies that were turned down many, many times before someone was able to see their potential and take the risk. We hope to reduce the risk by finding an audience beforehand.

Good writing and good luck!

Printed in Great Britain
by Amazon

27540357R00046